GW01167777

FRIDA KAHLO

2000 TASCHEN DIARY
www.taschen.com

Frida Kahlo (1907–1954)

The Mexican artist Frida Kahlo is one of the most important women painters of the 20th century, and one of the few Latin American artists to have achieved a global reputation. In 1983 her work was declared the property of the Mexican state.

Kahlo was the daughter of an immigrant German photographer and a Mexican woman of Indian extraction. Her life and work were more inextricably interwoven than in the case of almost any other artist. Two events in her life were of crucial importance. When she was eighteen, a bus accident put her in hospital for a year with injuries to her spine and a fractured pelvis. It was in her sick bed that she first started to paint. Then, aged twenty-one, she married the world-famous Mexican mural artist Diego Rivera. She was to suffer the effects of the accident her whole life long, and was particularly pained by her inability to have children. Her arresting pictures, most of them small-format self-portraits, express the burdens that weighed upon her soul: her unbearable physical pain, the grief that Rivera's occasional affairs prompted, the sorrow her childlessness caused her, her homesickness while living abroad; her longing to put down roots; and her profound loneliness. But they also declare her passionate love for her husband, her pronounced sensuousness, and her defiant will to live. Diego Rivera once described her work as being "as loveable as a beautiful smile and as cruel as all the bitterness of life".

Die Mexikanerin Frida Kahlo ist eine der bedeutendsten Malerinnen des 20. Jahrhunderts und zählt zu den wenigen weltbekannten Künstlern des südamerikanischen Kontinents. 1983 wurde ihr Werk zum mexikanischen Nationalbesitz erklärt.

Sie war die Tochter eines eingewanderten deutschen Fotografen und einer Mexikanerin indianischen Ursprungs. Wie bei kaum einem anderen Künstler sind bei ihr Leben und Werk eng miteinander verwoben. Zwei Ereignisse prägten ihre Biographie ganz besonders: Als sie 18 Jahre alt war, hatte sie einen schweren Busunfall und mußte mit zertrümmerter Wirbelsäule und gebrochenem Bein für ein Jahr ins Krankenhaus. Im Krankenbett begann sie zu malen. Mit 21 heiratete sie den weltberühmten mexikanischen Wandmaler Diego Rivera. Gegen die Folgen des Unfalls mußte sie ihr Leben lang ankämpfen. Besonders schmerzlich war für sie, daß sie keine Kinder bekommen konnte. In ihren eindringlichen Bildern – meist kleinformatige Selbstporträts – malte sich Frida Kahlo buchstäblich alles von der Seele: ihre unerträglichen körperlichen Schmerzen, ihren Liebeskummer wegen gelegentlicher Affären Diegos, ihre Trauer über die Kinderlosigkeit, das Heimweh im Ausland, die Sehnsucht nach Verwurzelung, ihre Einsamkeit, aber auch die leidenschaftliche Liebe zu ihrem Mann, ihre starke Sinnlichkeit und den trotzigen Überlebenswillen. „... liebenswert wie ein schönes Lächeln und grausam wie die Bitterkeit des Lebens ...", charakterisierte Diego Rivera einmal ihr Werk.

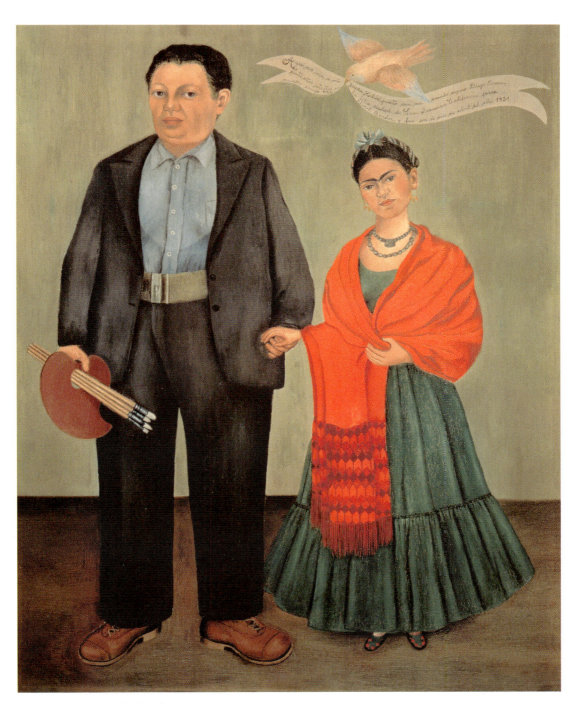

Frieda and Diego Rivera or **Frieda Kahlo and Diego Rivera**
1931. Oil on canvas, 100 x 79 cm
San Francisco, San Francisco Museum of Modern Art

Frida Kahlo (1907–1954)

La Mexicaine Frida Kahlo est l'un des peintres les plus marquants du XXᵉ siècle et compte parmi les rares artistes du continent sud-américain mondialement connus. Son œuvre est devenue la propriété de l'Etat mexicain en 1983.

   Fille d'un photographe allemand immigré et d'une Mexicaine d'origine indienne, elle associa très étroitement sa vie à son œuvre, comme bien peu d'autres artistes le firent. Deux événements ont tout particulièrement influencé le cours de sa vie : à l'âge de dix-huit ans, elle eut un grave accident d'autobus et dut passer un an à l'hôpital, la colonne vertébrale et le bassin brisés. Allongée sur son lit d'hôpital, elle commença à peindre. A l'âge de vingt et un ans, elle épousa le célèbre muraliste mexicain Diego Rivera. Toute sa vie, elle dut lutter contre les séquelles de l'accident. Il lui fut particulièrement douloureux de ne pas pouvoir avoir d'enfants. Dans ses tableaux percutants – la plupart du temps des autoportraits de petit formats –, elle peignit littéralement tout ce qu'elle avait sur le cœur : ses intolérables douleurs physiques, son chagrin d'amour dû aux liaisons occasionnelles de Diego, sa tristesse de ne pas pouvoir enfanter, la nostalgie de son pays quand elle séjournait à l'étranger, son désir d'enracinement, sa solitude, mais aussi son amour passionné pour son mari, sa vive sensualité et sa volonté acharnée de vivre. Diego Rivera déclara un jour que son œuvre était « ... engageante comme un beau sourire et cruelle comme l'amertume de la vie ... ».

De Mexicaanse kunstenares Frida Kahlo is een van de belangrijkste schilderessen van de 20e eeuw en bovendien een van de belangrijkste Zuid-Amerikaanse kunstenaressen die een internationale reputatie genieten. In 1983 werd haar werk eigendom van de Mexicaanse staat.

   Haar vader was een Duitse immigrant en fotograaf, en haar moeder een Mexicaanse van indiaanse oorsprong. Er zijn maar weinig kunstenaars van wie leven en werk zo nauw met elkaar verbonden zijn. Twee gebeurtenissen hebben Kahlo's leven totaal veranderd: op haar achttiende werd ze het slachtoffer van een busongeluk en belandde ze voor een jaar in het ziekenhuis met een verbrijzelde ruggengraat en een gebroken bekken. Op haar ziekbed begon zij met schilderen. Op eenentwintigjarige leeftijd trouwde ze met de bekende Mexicaanse muurschilder Diego Rivera. Haar hele leven heeft zij geleden onder de gevolgen van het busongeluk – ze kon hierdoor geen kinderen krijgen. In haar indringende schilderijen, veelal zelfportretten op klein formaat, schilderde ze over alles wat haar bezighield: haar ondraaglijke fysieke pijnen, haar verdriet over het overspel van Rivera en hun kinderloosheid, haar eenzaamheid en heimwee tijdens een verblijf in het buitenland en haar zoektocht naar stabiliteit. Maar de schilderijen geven ook blijk van een gepassioneerde liefde voor haar man en tonen haar sensualiteit en vastberadenheid om te overleven. Diego Rivera beschreef haar werk ooit als: "... lieflijk als een mooie glimlach en bitter als het leven zelf".

Pancho Villa and Adelita
before 1927. Oil on canvas, 65 x 45 cm
Tlaxcala, Instituto Tlaxcalteca de Cultura

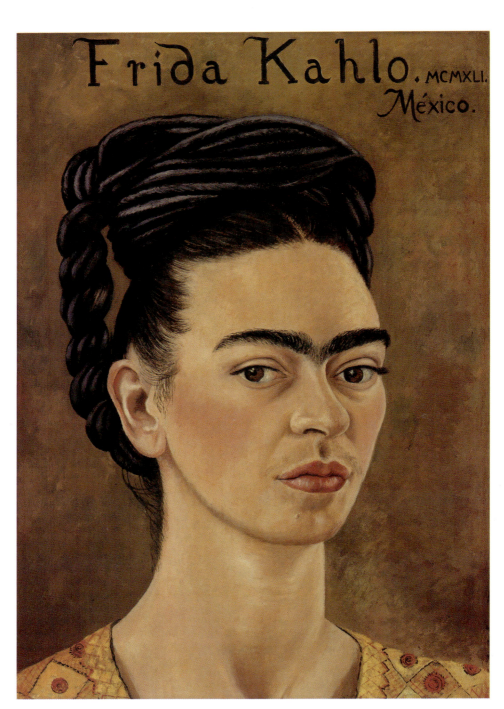

Self-portrait

1941. Oil on canvas, 39.5 x 29 cm

Mexico City, Collection Jacques & Natasha Gelman

Country Girl
before 1925. Watercolor and pencil on paper, 23 x 14 cm
Tlaxcala, Instituto Tlaxcalteca de Cultura

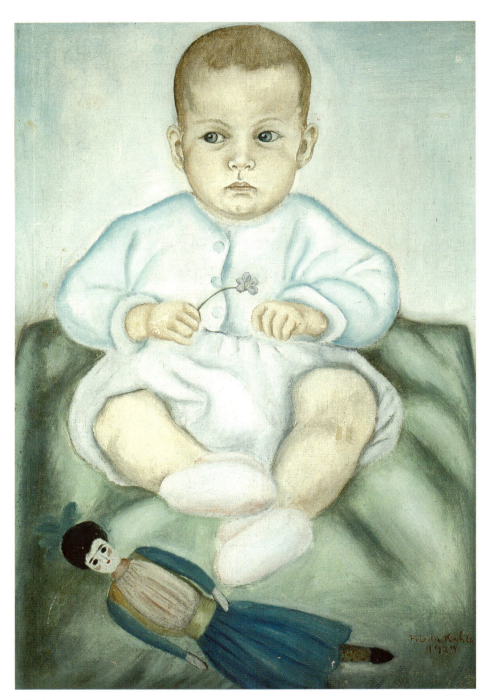

Girl in Diapers

1929. Oil on canvas, 65.5 x 44 cm

Mexico City, Collection Segúros América Banamex

Have Another One
before 1925. Watercolor and pencil on paper, 18 x 24.5 cm
Tlaxcala, Instituto Tlaxcalteca de Cultura

Portrait of Miguel N. Lira
1927. Oil on canvas, 99.2 x 67.5 cm
Tlaxcala, Instituto Tlaxcalteca de Cultura

Cantina Your Mother-in-Law
1927. Watercolor and pencil on paper, 18.5 x 24.5 cm
Private collection

Retrato de Mrs Jean Wight
pintado en Enero de 1931, en la ciudad
de San Francisco Cal. por Frieda Kahlo.

Portrait of Mrs. Jean Wight
1931. Oil on canvas, 63.5 x 46 cm
Private collection

Frida in Coyoacán
c. 1927. Watercolor on paper, 16 x 21 cm
Tlaxcala, Instituto Tlaxcalteca de Cultura

Luther Burbank

Portrait of Luther Burbank

1931. Oil on masonite, 86.5 x 61.7 cm

Mexico City, Collection Dolores Olmedo

Small Mexican Horse
c. 1928. Watercolor on paper, 27 x 33 cm
Mexico City, Collection Francisco González de la Vega

Portrait of a Lady in White
c. 1929. Oil on canvas, 119 x 81 cm
Private collection

Beauty Parlor (I) or **The Perm**
1932. Watercolor and pencil on paper, 26 x 22 cm
Mexico City, Collection Enrique Mereles

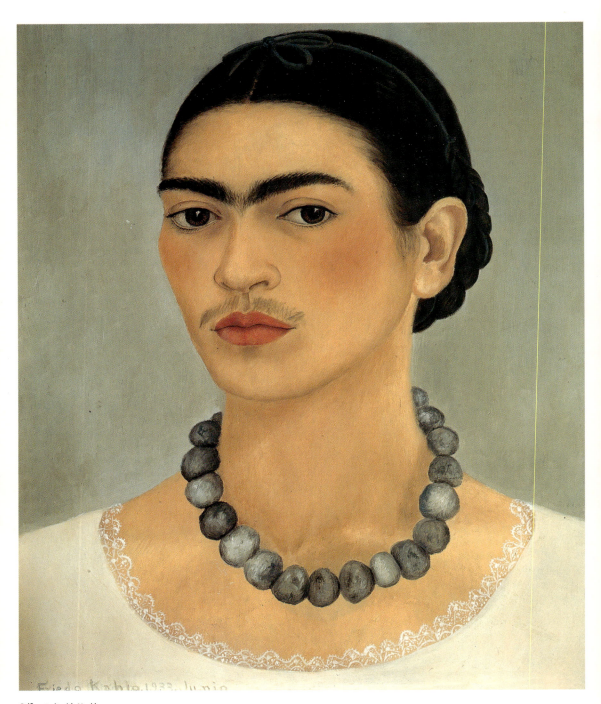

Self-portrait with Necklace
1933. Oil on metal, 34.5 x 29.5 cm
Mexico City, Collection Jacques & Natasha Gelman

My Grandparents, My Parents and I
1936. Oil and tempera on metal, 31 x 34 cm
New York (NY), Collection, The Museum of Modern Art,
Gift of Allan Roos, M. D. and B. Mathieu Roos

Self-portrait dedicated to Leon Trotsky or "Between the Courtains"
1937. Oil on canvas, 87 x 70 cm
Washington (D. C.), The National Museum for Women in the Arts

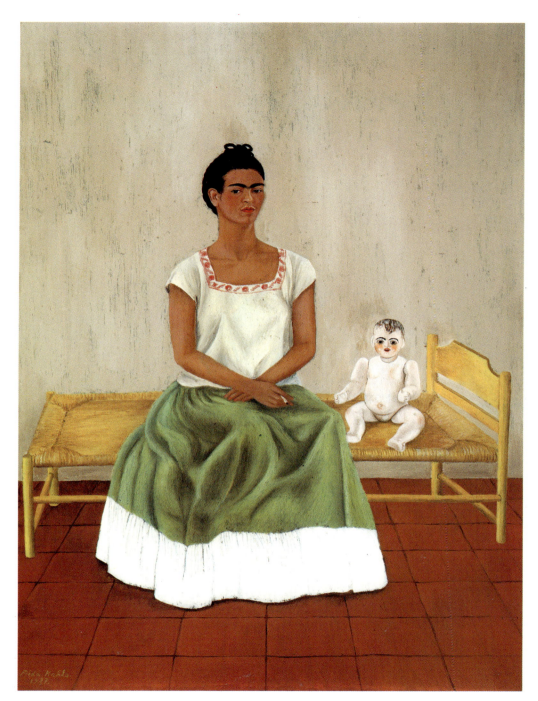

Self-portrait on the Bed or **Me and My Doll**
1937. Oil on metal, 40 x 31 cm
Mexico City, Collection Jacques & Natasha Gelman

Portrait of Alberto Misrachi
1937. Oil on metal, 34.5 x 27 cm
Mexico City, Collection Ana Misrachi

Portrait of Diego Rivera
1937. Oil on wood, 46 x 32 cm
Mexico City, Collection Jacques & Natasha Gelman

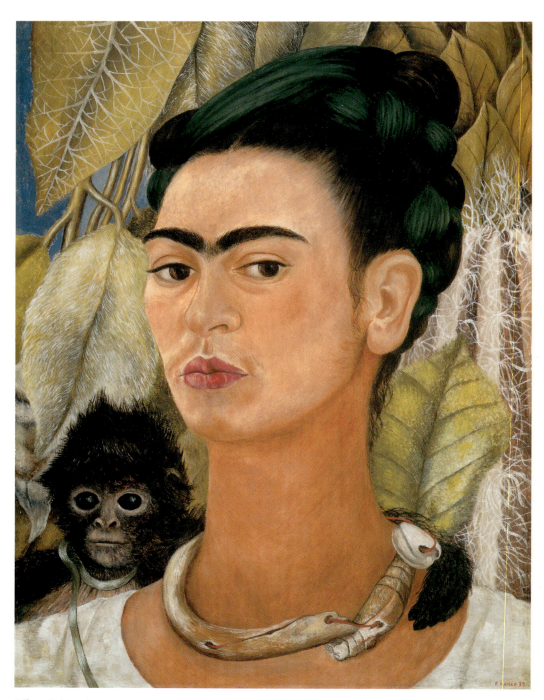

Self-portrait with Monkey
1938. Oil on masonite, 40.6 x 30.5 cm
Buffalo (NY), Albright-Knox Art Gallery,
Bequest of A. Conger Goodyear, 1966

Self-portrait "The Frame"
c. 1938. Oil on aluminium and glass, 29 x 22 cm
Paris, Musée National d'Art Moderne, Centre Georges Pompidou

Fruits of the Earth

1938. Oil on masonite, 40.6 x 60 cm

Mexico City, Collection Banco Nacional de México,
Fomento Cultural Banamex

Xochitl, Flower of Life
1938. Oil on metal, 18 x 9.5 cm
Mexico City, Collection Dr. Rodolfo Gómez

What I Saw in the Water or **What the Water Gave Me**
1938. Oil on canvas, 91 x 70.5 cm
Paris, Collection Daniel Filipacchi

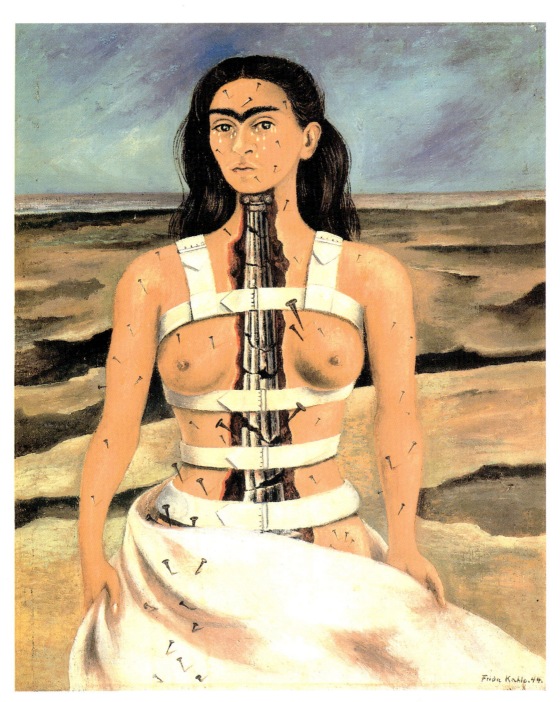

The Broken Column
1944. Oil on canvas, mounted on masonite, 40 x 30.7 cm
Mexico City, Collection Dolores Olmedo

Self-portrait with Small Monkey
1945. Oil on masonite, 57 x 42 cm
Cuernavaca, Collection Fundación Robert Brady

Untitled – Small Life (II)
c. 1928. Watercolor on paper, 18 x 25 cm
Collection Alejandro Gómez Arias

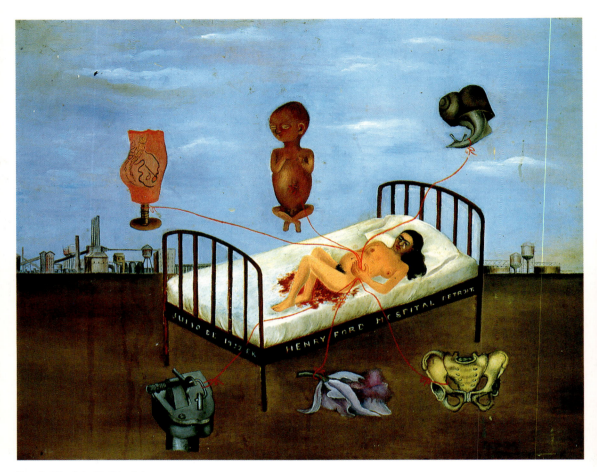

Henry Ford Hospital or **The Flying Bed**
1932. Oil on metal, 30.5 x 38 cm
Mexico City, Collection Dolores Olmedo

The Suicide of Dorothy Hale
1938/1939. Oil on masonite with painted wooden frame, 60.4 x 48.6 cm
Phoenix (AZ), Phoenix Art Museum

The Two Fridas
1939. Oil on canvas, 173.5 x 173 cm
Mexico City, Museo de Arte Mcderno

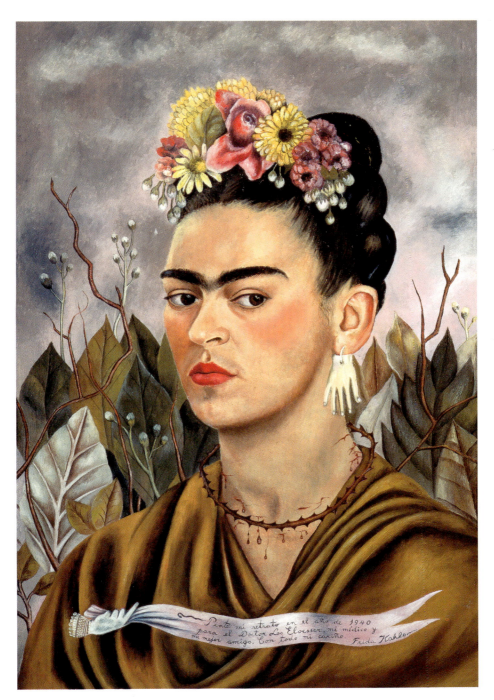

Self-portrait dedicated to Dr. Eloesser
1940. Oil on masonite, 59.5 x 40 cm
Private collection

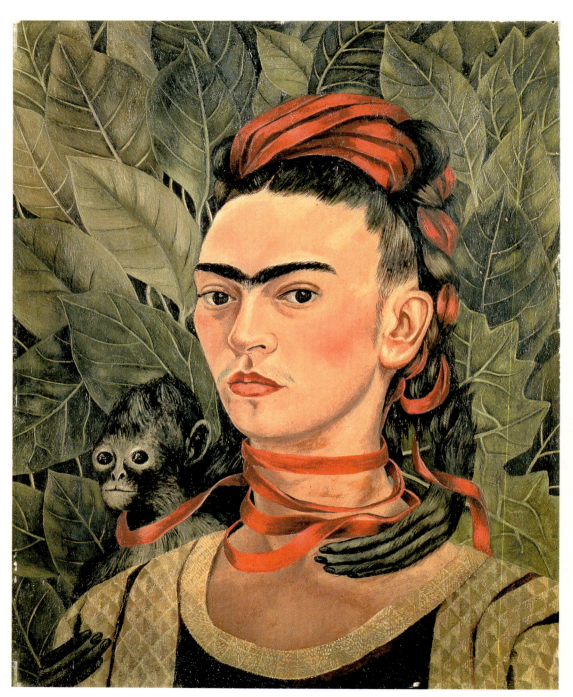

Self-portrait with Monkey
1940. Oil on masonite, 55.2 x 43.5 cm
Caracas, Collection Otto Atencio Troconis

Self-portrait with Braid
1941. Oil on masonite, 51 x 38.5 cm
Mexico City, Collection Jacques & Natasha Gelman

Soy de Samuel Fastlicht.
Me pinto con todo cariño,
Frida Kahlo, en 1951.
Coyoacán

Still Life
1951. Oil on canvas, mounted on masonite, 28.2 x 36 cm
Private collection

Retrato de la Sra. Marucha Lavín, lo pintó
Frida Kahlo. 1942.

Portrait of Marucha Lavín

1942. Oil on copper, diameter 65 cm

Mexico City, Collection José Domingo and Eugenia Lavín

Portrait of Lucha Maria, Girl from Tehuacán or **Sun and Moon** or **Woman with Wrap**
1942. Oil on masonite, 54.6 x 43.1 cm
Private collection

Self-portrait as a Tehuana or **Diego in My Mind** or **Thinking of Diego**
1943. Oil on masonite, 76 x 61 cm
Mexico City, Collection Jacques & Natasha Gelman

La novia que se espanta de ver la vida abierta.

The Bride Who Becomes Frightened When She Sees Life Open
1943. Oil on canvas, 63 x 81.5 cm
Mexico City, Collection Jacques & Natasha Gelman

Thinking of Death
1943. Oil on canvas, mounted on masonite, 44.5 x 36.3 cm
Private collection

Portrait of Natasha Gelman
1943. Oil on canvas, 30 x 23 cm
Mexico City, Collection Jacques & Natasha Gelman

Self-portrait with Monkeys
1943. Oil on canvas, 81.5 x 63 cm
Mexico City, Collection Jacques & Natasha Gelman

Portrait of Ing. Marte R. Gómez
1944. Oil on masonite, 32.5 x 26.5 cm
Mexico City, Collection Marte Gómez Leal

Diego and Frida 1929–1944 (I) or **Double Portrait of Diego and I (I)**
1944. Oil on masonite with shell surround, 26 x 18.5 cm (image: 12.3 x 7.4 cm)
Mexico City, Collection Francisco and Rosi González Vázquez

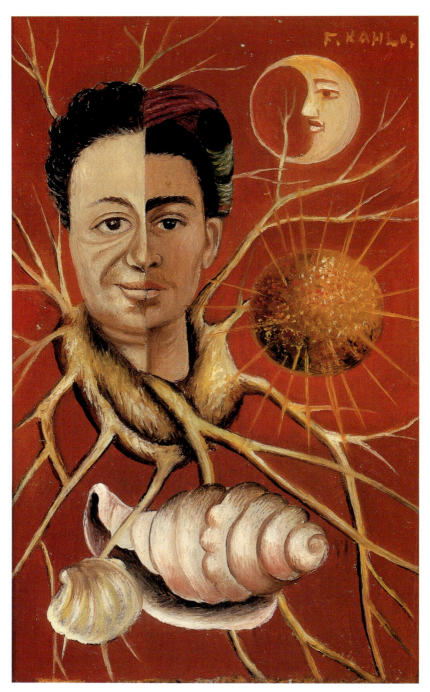

Diego and Frida 1929–1944 (II) or **Double Portrait of Diego and I (II)**
1944. Oil on masonite, 13.5 x 8.5 cm
Mexico City, Collection Maria Felix

Moses or **Nuclear Sun**

1945. Oil on masonite, 61 x 75.6 cm

Private collection

Self-portrait dedicated to Marte R. Gómez

1946. Pencil on paper, 38.5 x 32.5 cm

Private collection

Still Life
1952. Oil on canvas, mounted on wood, 25.8 x 44 cm
Private collection

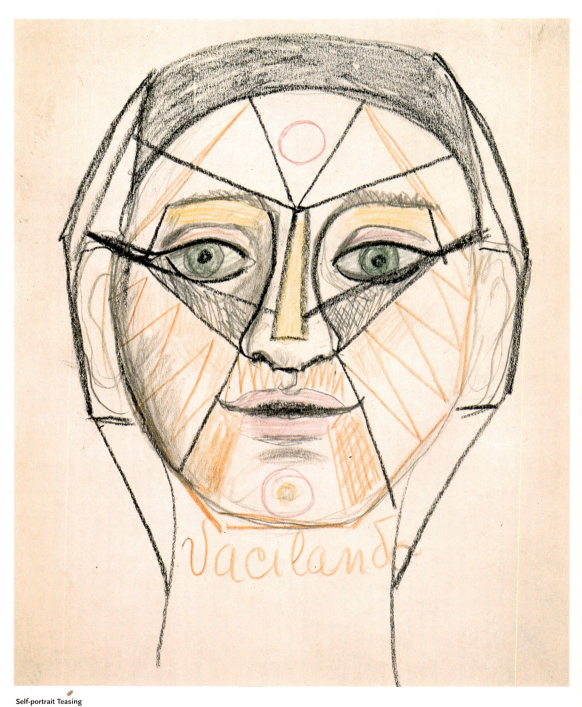

Self-portrait Teasing

c. 1946. Pencil and crayon on paper, 19.5 x 16 cm

Private collection

The Wounded Deer or **The Little Deer** or **I Am just a Poor Deer**
1946. Oil on masonite, 22.4 x 30 cm
Private collection

Sun and Life
1947. Oil on masonite, 40 x 50 cm
Mexico City, Galería Arvil

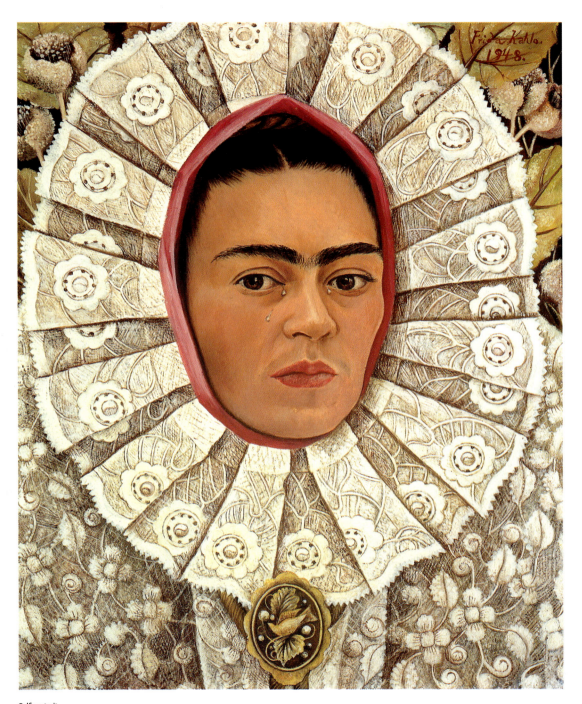

Self-portrait
1948. Oil on masonite, 50 x 39.5 cm
Private collection

The Love-Embrace of the Universe, the Earth (Mexico), Me, Diego and Mr. Xólotl
1949. Oil on canvas, 70 x 60.5 cm
Mexico City, Collection Jacques & Natasha Gelman

Still Life with Parrot and Flag
1951. Oil on masonite, 28 x 40 cm
Mexico City, Collection Diaz Ordaz

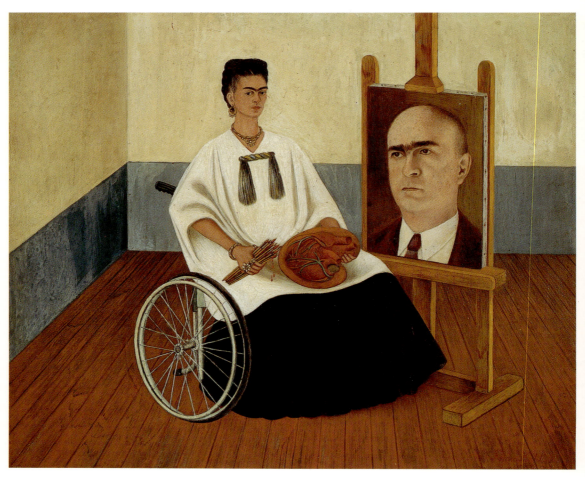

Self-portrait with Portrait of Dr. Farill or **Self-portrait with Dr. Juan Farill**
1951. Oil on masonite, 41.5 x 50 cm
Mexico City, Galería Arvil

Still Life with "Long Live Life"

c. 1951–1954. Oil on masonite, 39 x 65 cm
Private collection

US$ 16.99
ISBN 3-8228-6735-7

9 783822 867358